The Essential Guide for Self-Publishing

Top Tips for Before, During, and After Publication

By

Bryony Best

Copyright ©2024 by Bryony Best

All rights reserved. No part of this publication may be reproduced, stored or in any form of retrieval system or transmitted in any form or by any means without prior permission in writing from the publishers except for the use of brief quotations in a book review.

Paperback: 978-1-7392860-7-1

eBook: 978-1-7392860-8-8

Cover designer: Aethrastic Designs

Editor: Lucie O'Donnell

www.bryonybest.com

Chapters

Introduction

Chapter 1, Before Writing

Chapter 2, Publishing Contracts

Chapter 3, Legal Requirements & Copyright Law

Chapter 4, Tasks

Chapter 5, Publishing Avenues

Chapter 6, Social Media

Chapter 7, Marketing

Chapter 8, Helpful Advice

Chapter 9, My Secret

Introduction

Greetings fellow writer, my name is Bryony Best, and I am going to support you through the muddy path of self-publishing.

Who the hell am I?

I am nobody special, but I do have a particular set of skills and knowledge that can help springboard you forward into your author career.

Am I a genius? No.

Am I special? No. However, I do have an in-depth knowledge of self-publishing which I usually share with writers through my workshops and career coaching.

I believe that it is from my experience within business, marketing, and sales that assisted me on my journey to success. I published my first book in November 2021 and then followed this publication by releasing five more books, my own clothing line and book merchandise.

Am I a millionaire? I wish!

Can I help you? Yes, I can.

Three of my first six publications hit the bestseller list on Amazon, and my books are being used as resources within mental health in both the UK and USA.

In this book I will cover hot topics, technical tasks, sales techniques and my secret to success.

The real question is, ARE YOU READY?

Chapter 1

You have an idea for a book, and most advice would be to just write it. Get your laptop and notepad and just bash away and get your ideas out of your head, and into the screen.

This is good advice as you need to type up your book, however I don't just type my thoughts into my laptop. I think about a few important questions first.

Who will be my perfect audience or customer?

How will I sum the book up in a few sentences?

What is the hook for the book? A hook is the top selling point or what the reader will gain by reading the book.

The reason I ask myself these questions is because most social media platforms and avenues for sales will only allow a restricted number of words per posts. Readers, friends, and family will all ask you to tell them about your book. A few avid readers will allow you a minute or two, but the truth is you must be able to sum up your book and hook the reader into to buying it within a few words, or sentences.

Top social media sites, radio stations and TV appearances will usually ask for a quick summary of the book. It is hard to grab the attention of a customer and reel them in within a short space of time. If you, the author cannot sum up and sell your book within a quick sale pitch then why will they buy it?

Did you notice I am flitting between the word customer and reader? They are the SAME! Readers are customers who want to find their next book to love, you as the author will need to be able to sell your book both in person and digitally.

I am a writer NOT a salesperson!

I understood from the beginning that I would be required to pitch my book to shop owners, friends, and strangers. If this is something that you feel uncomfortable with then you have three options.

Find help to improve these necessary skills.

Be confident that you have thousands of pounds to spend on paying someone else to do it.

Go ahead anyway and hope for the best.

I do not place my dreams and goals in a basket of hope, I like facts and knowledge. I am lucky that I was a top salesperson many years ago, I am what they call a natural with the gift of the gab.

Another factor I consider before writing a new book is the impact and importance of my first sentence. Social media trends often post videos asking authors to share the first sentence of their book. Armed with this knowledge I started my thriller book with the following sentence. Blood trickled down the wall like treacle, pooling on the hard wood flooring like a tap dripping to its own beat.

I had no idea about this when I wrote my first novel, but I now use this to my advantage.

A similar statement can be said for the acknowledgement page, so I keep this in mind before I start tapping away at my keyboard.

The next point to consider is whether your book is themed or seasonal, this can help you decide on the best month to publish your book. For example, my poetry book was released at the end of September, a few days before National Poetry Day. This increased my chances of sales, and I knew that social media algorithms would be pushing poems and poetry related posts. If you have no understanding of trends and algorithms then have no fear, for I will cover this in a later chapter.

My published books are themed with mental health as a topic, lucky for me because humanity has never been more aware of the importance of looking after their own mental health. Therefore, the last point I consider is whether the topics or subjects within the book are popular or trending around the globe.

Some authors may add a subject or theme in hope of hitting a hot topic, this is called writing to market. The author writes based on trends and popular themes. This is not a guarantee for success. I personally do not write to market, but it is important to understand how similar books are performing in the genre you are keen to write in. Take Romance books as an example, if you were keen to write a similar book then I would suggest researching successful books to gain important knowledge, for this genre and area. I often search for books within my next genre of book to study successful cover designs and layouts. Imagine if you wrote a book about the anxiety and troubles of being a billionaire. Do you think there would be a big market for this book? With a current population of 8.2 billion humans on earth and yet only 2,781 of them are billionaires, I doubt this would be a wise move.

Chapter 2

You may have heard of Traditional Publishing, Self-Publishing, Hybrid or Vanity Publishing, or Independent Publishing which is also known as Indie Publishing.

I am going to break them down and give you a crash course in publishing avenues.

We will start off with **traditional publishing** as it is the one people think of when they dream of becoming a successful author. Traditional publishing is when an author accepts a contact from an agency or publishing house. The publisher usually takes on all the financial costs and therefore this is usually an attractive and realistic path for an author seeking a contract. The author is paid an advance up front and then offered a low percentage of royalty payments following on from book sales. The publisher would usually take full control of the book and marketing strategies. Sounds good, right? A few aspects to consider, is they hold all the rights and control, and they decide when your book will be released. Your book could end up at the back of a very long line of authors waiting for their own book to be published. The good side is that you if your books flops then you won't have lost any money. How much money the publisher puts into marketing depends on just how much success they believe your book to potentially hold.

Can you just approach a publisher?

Technically the answer is yes, but there are processes in place and formalities to uphold. First you will need to research publishing companies to find one that you would like to approach. You will need to ensure that they will accept queries from authors without an agent. A few publishers will only correspond with an agent, and some will only accept book queries at certain times of the year and for limited genres.

If you find a publishing company, they will have a how to guide for authors wanting to query them. Most publishers require an online form to be completed, with details about the book. They may also ask for the first few chapters as a sample. Once these steps have been completed you then start the waiting game. If you are lucky enough to hear back from them asking for more chapters, then a contract offer is looking more promising. The process from start to finish can take several months and this is just the beginning.

Does traditionally publishing my book mean that I will not be required to market and sell my book? Nope, you will still be required to attend marketing events and appearances. Plus, once the company hit their budget limit for marketing you may need to step in and take the reins. Of course, you may sell billions of books before this happens, but the statistics don't back this theory for first time or new authors.

If you decide you want to **self-publish** with a Self-Publishing company, then the same approach is required. However, you will be responsible for all financial costs. You will also have full control over decisions, content, cover design, and editing. This avenue usually comes with all the risk but also with full rewards. You will not receive an advance payment, but you will retain full royalty payments for all sales of the book. You will also be solely responsible for marketing and selling your book. Is this a big risk? Yes. I give advice to all authors to research their dream career and speak with others who have trodden this path. Successful authors who started off as your average newbie share their stories via social media, unveiling the truth behind the scenes of being a self-published or indie author. It can take many years of working multiple jobs before an author is successful enough to finance their rent and bills from their craft. Did you know that if you self-publish a book and a TV network or big entertainment company wants to turn it into a film or show that you own 100% of the rights?

It brings up the million-dollar question; of how much control or rights does an author in the same position have if they traditionally published their book?

What is a Vanity Publisher or Hybrid Contract? They follow the same module but are known for their different approaches, driven by their company core values. It is a contract that is not fully traditional and not quite self-publishing. This falls smack, bang, in the middle. They will usually offer to pay for fifty percent of the financial costs and therefore you will be responsible for the other fifty percent. They will own half the rights, and you will own the other half. The best thing is to read the contract offer carefully, because some may not stipulate how much the budget for marketing is. So, the idea of the marketing being paid for may just be a carrot that is not very long at all. In fact, they may offer as little as a few thousand pounds for marketing which is not sufficient for your needs at all. A few authors find this offer attractive for they may not be able to afford for a reputable self-publishing company to support them.

How much does self-publishing cost? Great question. You could be expected to pay anything from £500 up to

£3,000. And yes, you sometimes get what you pay for! The cheapest is not always the best. The positive would be that an established self-publishing company will have expert staff who can support you through the whole process, my advice would be to choose wisely. I self-published my first two books and I was incredibly lucky to stumble across the United Kingdom's number 01 bestselling self-publishing company.

For the final contract we will discuss **indie publishing** also known as independent publishing. Many authors are overwhelmed with the tasks and requirements for indie publishing, but their desire to publish outweighs their never-ending task list. As an independent publisher you will either find or learn how to do the following. You can either teach yourself or hire someone else to do the below.

Edit and proofread the book, design a cover and format the cover and book layout. Purchase ISBNs and upload the book. You will be responsible for planning, design, decisions, accounts, purchasing, marketing, researching, finding arc readers, legal requirements, your website, and all content.

You will hire and pay others for their services; and you will also need to create author accounts for any sites or avenues where you wish to publish your book. This is certainly more responsibility than most contracts or avenues to publish are, but it gives you full control.

How much does it cost? How long is piece of string! It depends on who you hire and what you are willing to pay. I have paid less than fifty pounds for a cover design, but I have also paid hundreds of pounds for a similar service.

You will need to decide which avenue is best suited to you and your needs. Only you will know the answers to this question. I will share with you how and why I chose said avenues for my own publications. I sent queries for my first book, and I received a reply from an interested party. I was asked to send more chapters of my book by a deadline. I missed the deadline due to personal reasons. Many years later when I again wanted to publish the book, I researched self-publishing companies and found the best one in the UK. After I sent them my query, they supported me to publish my book, and I still had no expectations of massive sales. The book was a big hit, and this gave me the incentive to write another book, which I did not have the finances to pay for. My first book cost me £2,600 to publish and I also launched my own merchandise which gave me greater return financially. I sent queries for my second book to five publishing companies who all offered me a contract. Once I read the contract I decided to decline their offers. They either offered little marketing budgets, or they didn't stipulate an amount. My books are based on my life, with this in mind I feared that handing over any control could be catastrophic. I returned to my self-publisher company and published my second book with them. My second book hit the Amazon bestseller list within twenty-four hours of its release! This same book is consistently in the top 100 on Amazon, long after and a few years on from its original release date. My further publications have all been indie published, this is due to finances. I simply couldn't wait for the return of royalties before releasing my next books. It was far from easy, I watched videos and taught myself how to format, upload and publish books. I can now publish a book for £500 and this offers me great opportunities to release book after book with no time issues or financial constraints. I will share more information and tips for independently publishing throughout this book. I currently have paid for cover designers and adverts, I have also used free cover designers, all which will be explained further in the relevant chapters.

Chapter 3

What are the legal requirements for publishing a book?

Laws may differ depending on which country you are in, for any book published with an ISBN in the UK you will need to send a free copy to the Great British Library in London.

What is an ISBN?

The ISBN is a unique number assigned to your book, you will notice the number inside the book, and it is usually embedded into the barcode. You can purchase ISBNs in the UK from Nielsen, which country you reside in will decide where you can attain them. For example, in America there is an agency you can purchase them from.

Can you use a free ISBN or no ISBN? Yes, if you decide to publish your book with the sole intention of only selling the book yourself, an ISBN wouldn't be required. Keep in mind that shops and online stores will only sell books with an ISBN. You may opt to use a free ISBN from certain publishing sites, but the downside is that you can only use that ISBN on their site. If you wanted to publish your book through multiple avenues, then you wouldn't be able to use the free ISBN on any other site. In conclusion an ISBN is not a legal requirement to publish but it is essential if you want worldwide distribution for sales through retailers.

Once you have published a book with an ISBN you may receive an email with a few demands for free books under the Legal Deposit Law. Is it a legal requirement for you to send free copies of your books to national libraries? Yes, they can ask for you to send X number of books to the legal deposit department. In the UK we are usually asked for five copies of the book, if the email is sent within one of year of publication, then it is the law. The law is in place to preserve the knowledge for future generations. I must confess it feels pretty good to be included in this, and I was happy to send them copies. I would suggest you research this law for your own country to ensure you are legally compliant.

Copyright Law

In the UK copyright is free and all your work is protected by these laws. It is common practice to add a copyright statement in your book, you can easily search for the wording or look inside a book for an example. Again, I would suggest that you research this if your county is outside the UK.

Can you add quotes and references in your book?

This is a common question, and I will try and keep my answer as simple as possible. Some literature is in the public domain therefore you may be able to easily add it to your book. Public domain work is not owned or patented by an individual. In the UK a creator's work can be made public domain seventy years after their death. These laws vary from country to country. If you wish to quote a person or company, then you will need their permission. You can reference others work or publications, but as the copyright law states, only use of short quotes for reviews is allowed. You will need to research any quotes or text that is not owned by you and add the date and name of any quotes that you reference.

You can access cover designs and pictures that are free from copyright via many different avenues.

Your work is also protected under copyright law, it is important that you understand the correct process for copyright infringement.

How does this effect you?

A disgusting fact is that authors are often pirated, I have been subjected to this on many occasions. I was informed that this is a sign that I have made it. It did not feel like a good sign, it felt more like a stab to the heart to have my books ripped off by a stranger. I have found sites pretending to be the author of my publications and they were making money by illegally selling digital copies of my books. I have also found sites for cover designers with my book covers in their portfolio, pretending to have designed my covers.

What is the correct next step?

You send the site owner a legal take down notice, that is all you can do. You can search for templates of this letter on the internet if you wish to learn about the document. I have sent emails to sites and informed them that they have users who are breaking copyright laws, the site owner has then removed the user who was breaking the law. A big example of this is a pirating site that has gone to battle with BIG publishing companies and after a long fight the illegal site was removed. A few days later the same site appeared back in business but under a different company name. Book pirating is very common so ensure you are protected. I personally signed up to a piracy protection site which search day and night for pirated copies of my books, if they find one they then send the legal take down notice letter. I can add different book titles and keep track of pirating. Another form of copyright issues I have encountered is with my book merchandise and company logo. There are many people who are not aware of or respect copyright laws, in fact I have spotted clothing and merchandise with my logo on them. People can easily download pictures and logos from your social media sites and then use them to create items to sell. My advice is to not use your best resolution photos on social media. To explain this further the resolution needed for a book cover or logo is usually X amount, if you wish to blow up the image to make a large roller banner or beach towel the image will be distorted and not suitable. I have photos of my books which can be enlarged to make merchandise, but I also have smaller resolution book covers that are not suitable for enlarging. I try and use my lowest resolution photos across my social media accounts.

In a further chapter we will discuss marketing and newsletters. For the benefit of this section please ensure you are aware of the data protection laws when storing other people's data. When an author has a newsletter list of recipients it is vital they follow the privacy and protection laws. For example, when sending emails make sure you BCC the email addresses, to ensure you do not accidently share anyone's email address. All data must be stored, and password protected. When sharing videos and photos of your author tasks make sure you do not breach anyone's personal data or identity, this can be accidently done if recording a video of postage that may have an address on it.

You may wish to create a legal contract when working with others, for example illustrators, editors, and any other service that requires others having access to your work.

You may be required to sign a legally binding contract with a publishing company, always seek legal advice if you are unsure of any legal requirements.

Chapter 4

Here is a list of tasks that we will discuss further, Proof Reading, Editing, Formatting, File Types, Arc and Beta readers, Cover Design, and Blurbs.

The above tasks are required before you publish your book. I have purposely left out marketing as that task has its very own chapter.

If you use a self-publishing company, then most of the above will be handled for you. They will consult with you throughout, but they will have a team of experts who will complete each task. They will usually calculate a cost for these services based on your book word count. If your book is over fifty thousand words then it qualifies as a novel, under this is known as a novella. A short story is between one thousand and ten thousand words. Any writing under one thousand words is known as flash fiction.

Proof Reading

This is the process of someone else checking your writing for mistakes. You as the author will complete this task many times. Proof reading is searching for grammar and spelling errors. You may pay someone to do this or use a competent friend or colleague.

Editing

Is the step known to change, adapt and reword any text. This is with the goal for improving the writing and story. Some professionals will remove words that are believed to be not needed or a word to avoid. If you are writing a book that has a high word count, then you may wish to remove unnecessary words to improve the book and to reduce the word count. The final page count of your book adds to the printing cost, which makes the font size and formatting an important job. Font size and type is important, you may wish to research commonly used styles and font size based on your genre or ideal customer. For example, my book sales data demonstrated that majority of my readers were over the age of forty, with this in mind I published my fourth book with a font size of eleven. My first three books were published with a smaller font. I made this decision based on customer feedback at events, readers informed me that they preferred the slightly bigger font size. My fifth book was originally planned to be published in the larger font size, but after calculating the print cost I reduced the font size to make it cheaper to print each book.

Formatting & File Types

Publishing sites will stipulate which type of files they will accept, from PDF versions to EPUB and others. If you are uploading a book cover or the inside pages of a book, you need to use the recommended file type. Digital copies of your book will be read on many different size devices which is why the file type is vital as it allows the book size and pages to adapt to different reading devices.

Many sites have free tools, an area where you can create a template for your book cover design. You will need to create this template to either use yourself or to send to the cover designer. You cannot make this template until you have a final word count, because the number of pages of your book will determine the cover size needed.

Formatting is an area that I used to fear, it is the layout of the book, and it is vital you get this step right. When you upload a book to be published and printed it needs to be in the correct format. This is everchanging so you will need to keep up to date with the requirements. For example, if I upload an e-book then you do not add page numbers. When I upload a book the correct margin sizes and guttering needs to be correct for the book size. First you decide the book size, then you add the margin and guttering size. You can set these before you start writing or after you have finished the book. I prefer to set these before I start typing. The margin is the gap between the sentence and the edge of the page, with a top, bottom, and side margins. The print layout can be set to mirroring which means the left and right page mirror each other's setting. The guttering is especially important for books over fifty thousand words, it is the amount of space you allow for the pages to meet in the spine. If you did not add a guttering and you printed a large word count book you risk some of the sentences starting in the spinal area which the readers could not physically read. When you finish writing a chapter you will want to add page break rather than skipping to the next page, this page breaks controls where a page ends and a new page begins. If you upload an e-book and you do not add page break, then your chapters will look sloppy, and you may have a new chapter starting halfway down the previous chapters page. Formatting is organising the data for the computer to read; this needs to be correct for many computer programs and printers will process this information to print your book. Readers will judge you for poor formatting and many complaints could be made. When a reader finishes a book they can report poor formatting, which could result in the suspension of your book sales until you rectify the issues raised. A professional looking book will be received better by readers, and this is vital for continued sales and good reviews.

Cover Design

If you have the correct programs and skills, you may choose to design your own book cover. If like me, you are clueless then you may want to hire a book cover designer. A third option would be to use a free book cover created on a publishing site. If you publish a book on multiple sites, they may require a slightly different sized cover design despite the fact the book is the same size on both sites. I assume this is to cause annoyance and I usually pay for the same designed book cover for various sizes depending on which publishing sites I use. You will firstly need to know the final word count and page number for your book. This information alongside the book size is usually needed for you to create a book cover design template. If you are releasing a short book, less than X number of pages then you may forfeit the option for a spinal section, most authors add their name and book title to the spinal collum. My poetry book is only thirty pages so therefore it does not have a spine big enough to print on. The design for the front cover and back cover is one design. Many sites will add the barcode with the ISBN details for free to the cover when it is printed. The blurb is added to the back cover, and the book title and subtitle with authors name is added to the front page. You could add a picture of yourself to the back page, the design is your decision. I research similar books that are selling well for tips and advice for a suitable cover. You can use photos for your cover design too, the choice is yours. I have paid others to create my book cover and opted for them to make me promotional graphics. I use promotional graphics to promote the book before and after it is published. I have also used the free cover designs on two separate publishing sites, the downside being that I did not have a photo of the front cover, back cover, or promotional pictures to use for marketing. When you pay a cover designer, they will send you the designs and graphics created to use across your social media sites or for marketing purposes. When you hire a designer, they will usually offer unlimited changes to the cover design to help you find the perfect cover, but that does not include any design stipulations that were not agreed upon for the original requirement. For example, I could ask a designer to change the picture of a shell to be smaller, bigger, or a different colour. I could not ask them to swap a shell and change my mind completely for a new object. You may find a designer who is more flexible, but the most common process is for you the author to stipulate a basic idea or requirement for the cover and then continue based on the original idea. Keeping to the original cover design idea is common practice when you hire a professional, or when working with a self-publishing company.

Arc and Beta Readers

Authors send their book to avid readers for feedback before a book is released, this could also be done by carefully selected friends or colleagues. I personally used a few close friends that I trust, I choose which people to use based on their knowledge and skill set. For example, when I was writing my second book, I was worried that readers of different knowledge levels for spiritualism could read the book. I wanted the book to be clear and understood by readers with different levels of knowledge. To counteract this fear, I selected three friends to be arc readers, they read each chapter after I finished writing it and then they gave me feedback. I chose friend A because she had lots of knowledge for spiritualism, I chose friend B because she had never heard of spiritualism, and friend C was chosen because she had a little knowledge. This helped me gage reader feedback and their understanding of technical jargon described in the book. Many authors will promote their book by advertising for arc or beta readers, they then send a free copy of the book for them to read and give feedback on. The author should be very careful as some readers may take their work and share it on pirating sites. Authors should take suitable steps to avoid this. The readers then can add their reviews to official sites on the books release date, increasing reviews early on. The readers are usually selected if they have large social media followings, and they agree to share their reviews across their social sites which also helps books sales and promotion. The first time a book is sent out to readers to review, and feedback is called the arc group, the adapted or revised copy would then be sent to the next group called the beta group. Arc stands for an advance copy of an unpublished book.

Blurb

Most authors find this the hardest part to write, I however find it easy. The blurb is the section on the back cover that gives readers an understanding of what the book is about. Some authors add quotes about the book from newspapers or specific people, with permission from the person or company in question. I am a reader, so I read a blurb I have created and ask myself, would I want to read this book based on the blurb?

Another tip that may help you write your blurb or choose a title is again to research. Look at top selling books and see which buzz words they are using within their own blurbs. You can up your game and find out what customers are typing into search engines to discover new books. I have a friend who does this for me, I give him the book genre and subject and he does a search. After he collates the results, he tells me which words and sentences customers are typing to find similar books. I then use this data to ensure these key words are in my blurb and description.

Chapter 5

There are various avenues to publish your book through, new websites and platforms are arising daily. My advice would be to research them for an up-to-date list. We will discuss the most popular avenues for self-publishing which are Print Only, Ingram Spark, and KDP.

KDP is the shortened name for Kindle Direct Publishing, better known as Amazon. I will break down some of the popular pros and cons for each site, however they are ever changing and adapting to author feedback.

When I first published a book both Ingram Spark and KDP offered great benefits and incentives for using them to publish my books. KDP was, and still is free to use and upload your book onto. Ingram Spark charged a fee for uploading books but have since eliminated this fee. Both sites can publish digital, paperback, and hardback.

KDP is known for offering a service for authors to sign their books up to, called Kindle Unlimited. Readers pay a monthly subscription fee for having access to e-books, rather than paying for each individual one. The author is paid by KDP after they calculate how many pages of the authors e-book/s are read by readers.

KDP and Ingram Spark both make payments in arrears, meaning the author is paid in April for book and e-book sales from three month earlier. I assume this is because they calculate sales from all over the globe.

I have never signed up to Kindle Unlimited despite the wonderful opportunity for my books to be accessed by masses of readers, who may also review the book. I have always been too scared. I know of authors who have sadly been pirated and therefore it effected their accounts with Kindle Unlimited. An e-book on Kindle Unlimited is only useful and attractive to the publishing site if the reader cannot access the book for free elsewhere. There are many authors who do sign their e-book up to Kindle Unlimited and they receive many new readers and reviews because of it. My books are under 70,000 words, with this in mind I did not feel that being paid for page reads would be the best approach for my books.

The good news is that you do not have to sign up to Kindle Unlimited, the choice is yours. Publishing with KDP is free, and you have access to all their publishing tools. Amazon print and sell books all over the world, making your readers access worldwide. You can choose to publish either a print copy or digital, I usually opt for both formats. The platform to upload and set up your new book is user friendly and easy to navigate. KDP offer a free ISBN service but remember that you can only use the free ISBN on their site. I purchase my own ISBNs, and this allows me to use the same ISBN for the same book when I publish it through both KDP and Ingram Spark.

Creating an author account with KDP is straight forward and this will require an email address and common set up information. Banking details will be required for payments to be made to you from Amazon. You can add information about yourself to your author account which allows customers to follow you on Amazon, which is excellent for marketing. Followers will be sent emails when you release a new book.

KDP require book covers and the book content to be uploaded in certain file formats. We touched on this in an earlier chapter when we discussed that e-books can be read across multiple devices, which is why a file type that allows for your book size and information to adapt to different devices is essential. The file formats change as technology evolves, I currently use EPUB files for my e-books, but KDP prefer KPF files at this current time. The inside of the book can be in the file type PDF. Remember, technology changes, therefore so does the required file type. You can easily research any changes when you are ready to publish your book.

KDP also sells audio books which readers can purchase, they allow authors to hire voice actors, and you can pay them by giving them a percentage of the audio book royalties. I have never used this service, but I am aware of authors who have. Paying a voice actor up front can cost a pretty penny, plus you would need access to a studio if they didn't have one themselves. You can choose to record your own audio books but ensure you do your homework, you will need access to a soundproof space, the correct technology and computer programs. It is not as simple as hitting the record button, the volume of the recordings must be within a specific range to guarantee it will play well across different outlets. The good news is that KDP have this option should you ever wish to pursue it.

To summarise the pros of publishing with KDP, they are free, with many free tools, access to audio book publishing, customers and sales worldwide, they print the books too, and they offer an advertisement service.

What is not so attractive, they take a high percentage for their services. Some authors complain about the print quality of any books ordered; however, I have never had an issue with any author copies that I have order.

Any local bookstores that agree for you to drop off copies of your book to sell, are likely to not want books printed by Amazon. When I order author copies from KDP I use them for selling at events, competitions or giveaways. If I need author copies printed to sell in shops, I order copies from Ingram Spark who are more expensive to order author copies from. The higher the price of the books the more your profit margin reduces. Shops can order copies of your book to sell themselves and when they do this, they usually order them from an official supplier like Ingram Spark. Retailers do not and cannot order copies of your book from KDP at a business rate to sell them to customers.

Ingram Spark publishing gives you the opportunity to upload and print your book without pushing the book out into worldwide distribution. This would mean you are using them more as a printing service rather than a publishing service. You wouldn't need an ISBN for your book, and you alone would need to sell and distribute your book.

They do offer a worldwide distribution service which would require your book to have an ISBN. You can upload e-book, hardback, and paperback versions. Once your book is published it will be added to their catalogue and pushed out across the world for sale across 40,000 retailers, schools, independent bookshops, e-book retailers, universities, and libraries. When bookshops want to order books to sell in their store they seek books via the Ingram Spark catalogue. There is a certain large bookshop here in the UK alongside supermarkets that have their books supplied, selected, and stocked by Gardners Books. When I publish with Ingram Spark my books are automatically available to Gardners as they are one of the 40,000 distribution routes via Ingram Spark.

Creating an author account is easy with Ingram Spark, but uploading books is slightly more difficult to navigate. Their process for checking your book before a digital proof copy is available takes longer than KDP. On KDP a basic file and format check takes up to three minutes, yet Ingram Spark check it all manually so it can take a few days for a digital proof copy to be emailed to you. On KDP a basic check is done then the book is subjected to a further check manually after you have submitted your book as being ready for publishing.

If you decide to publish your book through both sites, then ensure you read the user agreement to avoid any conflicts. When you publish your book through Ingram Spark one of their 40,000 distribution avenues are Amazon. If a copy of the book is already for sale on Amazon through KDP then they will not sell your book on there because a version of it will already exists for sale via Amazon.

Why publish through KDP if Ingram Spark can sell your book through the Amazon site?

I choose to publish with KDP as I receive majority of my book sales through KDP, and they give me a higher return financially than Ingram Spark. Ingram Spark offer the option to set a 70% royalty rate, but the printing cost is higher than KDP, and the retailers will not buy my books from Ingram Spark if I only offer them 30%. The reality is that I set my royalty at 45% to allow 55% discount to retailers via Ingram Spark. I still publish through Ingram Spark as it distributes my book through their 40,000 distributors. Also, on Ingram Spark you are required to choose a return setting for your book for sales based on the country it is sold in. For example, will you allow returned unsold books from retailers? Would you want any customer returned books to be destroyed or returned to you? If books are returned to you then this will incur a cost. If a retailer returns fifty books after you have been paid for the sale of fifty books, then you will owe money rather than being paid money. If you choose the no return option will retailers still order your books to sell? These are questions that you must decide on. What discount percentage will you offer retailers for stocking your book? Certain countries will not print and supply your book unless the discount fee ensures them a certain profit return.

An interesting piece of information is that Ingram Spark and KDP do not have the exact same book categories. When you are setting the book genre you will also be asked for other sub genres or categories. The two different publishing sites do not mirror each other. For example, I have a book published on one site under the category Thriller and Mystery, but on the other site it is set as a Psychological Thriller. The genre and sub genres help the site decide where to place your book, and it can assist bookshops and readers when they are searching for a particular type of book. It is important to select your keywords carefully when you are uploading your book. In an earlier chapter we discussed the option of researching keywords by reading blurbs for other successful books in the same genre. I use a friend who has a computer program that does this for me, arming me with the exact keywords customers type into search engines when they are looking for a certain type of book.

Print Only

You may choose a printing company to print your book and then you can sell it yourself. Keep in mind that official retailers will not sell books without an ISBN. And you alone will need to sell and distribute your own book. Printing costs can be high, and this will reduce your profit margin.

We have discussed profit margins a few times, I feel it is best to give you a real example.

Book X is set for sale on KDP at £9.99 and when it sells, I receive £3.48 per paperback sold in the UK. If it is sold in a different country, then the royalty adjusts based on the printing cost. KDP have subtracted the print cost and then their fee.

If I order an author copy from KDP it cost me £2.48, if I sell that book at £9.99 at an event then I have made £7.51. This does not include the cost of the table at the event, a wage to me to pay for my time, petrol to get there, and the cost of the free bookmark and keyring that I gave the customer.

If I order the same book from Ingram Spark, it cost me £2.68 per copy. My author copies cost more to buy from Ingram Spark.

Both sites also charge a delivery fee, this also must be taken into consideration.

I do not sell author copies of my book until it has reached the bestseller list on Amazon.

Why not?

Any author copies sold are excluded from any sale data, this includes your sale ranking on Amazon/KDP. As an author you want your sales to all be counted to increase your ranking, it is a great selling point if your book reaches the top 100 on Amazon. This is why I only sell author copies of my books once they have reached the bestseller list! Any author copies of your books that you sell are not included in any official sale data. Book sale rankings are achieved by books sold by the sites you published them through, and their official distributors.

Local stores that you personally approach with author copies of your book to stock and sell will usually want 35% of the book sale, that is before profit! If you sell a book for £10.00, they will want 35% of £10.00, leaving you £6.50. If the book was £3 for you to order and to have delivered, then your profit becomes £3.50. If you drove a car to deliver the book to the local shop, then you will need to minus that cost too. If you agree to this then you will want to create a SOR invoice, this is your evidence for how many books you have left at the shop. The invoice is for Sale or Return, if the books are not sold before the selected date, then the shop returns them. If any books have sold, then they are required to pay you the agreed amount. Obviously, if the shop buys your books directly from Ingram Spark, then you are paid your set royalty.

The royalty is set at a certain percentage, the aspects that effect it are, the page count of the book, physical book size, individual paper weight selected, the front and back cover finish, pictures in the book, the printing cost, and the distribution fee. These aspects effect the royalty, and the country of the book sale also has an effect. For example, Ingram Spark will print your book via various printing companies around the world so the print cost will always fluctuate. Money currency exchange rate is ever changing too. You, the author will choose the paper colour, weight and size. You will decide whether to print pictures inside your book when you upload your book. The last factor to consider is you have the option to choose which country you feel will have the most sales. If your e-book meets the set criteria you can set your royalty at 70% for sales made of digital book copies sold in your selected country. In other countries your royalty for e-book sales will be much less. This option is only available via KDP.

Chapter 6

Social Media posting can feel like you're throwing a dart into the ocean, but social media platforms can be a great tool if used correctly.

When should an author open accounts to post about their book?

As soon as possible, it can take years to build your following and find your ideal readers.

I have built my accounts organically, gaining true followers and potential customers. I have never purchased followers as I believe this would be a waste of time. Yes, you will want your accounts to look healthy and popular but only real followers will purchase your book. I had never been on Instagram, Twitter, Tik Tok or LinkedIn before I published my first book. In the past I had family and friends who run business accounts across popular sites for me. I was a newbie, and it was my close friend Emma who set up my Twitter account which is now called X.

Good advice usually given to new authors is for them to sign up to one or two social media platforms and to concentrate all their effort on them. I love a challenge, so I signed up for many.

Only you will know what you are capable of, so it is your decision how many platforms you decide to post on. I am signed up to Facebook, Instagram, Tik Tok, LinkedIn, Bookbub, Goodreads, Snapchat, Bookroar, X, and a few others.

How did I grow my accounts to over fifty thousand followers within a few short years?

I researched the sites I was using, and I joined them as a reader. While I used these social media sites, I learnt which videos performed well on each site. I started mimicking videos that I engaged with, and I followed accounts that offered advice for new authors. I quickly learnt that each platform has its own agenda, and they all follow algorithms. For example, for a short time Tik Tok was pushing out six second videos to viewers. I created six second videos, and my views and engagement started to rise. Instagram users are more interested in aesthetically pleasing photos, with this in mind I often use objects and decorations when taking a photo for Instagram. Every site favour original content, they do not like a video posted on their site which has evidence that the video was posted elsewhere first. For anyone who doesn't already know this, when you post a video to a site your name also known as a handle appears in the video with a symbol that represents the social media platform. You can use certain apps that remove the evidence of the original site symbol and handle name, allowing you to post the same video freely across all your social media sites.

I cannot explain every ounce of knowledge I have for algorithms because the sites change them frequently. I can share a few examples that are true today but may not be true when you read this book. Social media platforms desire engagement and they favour comments on posts consisting of five words and more. Posts that are shared are desired as they reach a further audience. Facebook favour a reaction to a post rather than just a thumbs up like. Instagram has just added a new feature called Notes, they will favour users who are using their new feature. It may sound confusing and everchanging but once you are using these sites you can experiment with posts and discover what works well for you.

I have followers who are interested in my books and the subject matters, I also have followers who are authors seeking my videos that offer free advice. A few followers maybe friends or family, who hopefully support my dreams and aspirations. I adore all my followers, and I am grateful for them. I especially like my committed fans who engage with my posts, which helps my posts reach a bigger audience.

If you are already using some of the popular sites for authors and readers, then you already have a head start. I started from scratch with no knowledge, I did my research, and I practiced until I discovered which posts work well for me. I would suggest you start these accounts as soon as possible; I was less fortunate, and I began my journey on social media just three months before my first book release.

Bookroar is a wonderful site that rewards readers with credits for reading and reviewing books, of course you must post the reviews across certain sites to gain the credit. Authors can then use the credits to add their own books to the selection pool for readers to choose from. This means you can gain more reviews for your books and help your book grow its audience. Did you know that less than 3% of readers leave a review? Authors need reviews as it helps other readers to decide whether to purchase a book or not. Amazon supports books by advertising them across emails to customers, when a book reaches a certain number of reviews. If you have two books which are the same, with the only difference being the number of reviews each book has, the one with the higher number of reviews will usually be given a higher ranking. Every author dreads a bad review, but we all get them. It is not the end of the world, but a good way to avoid a bad review due to a disappointed customer is to ensure you market your book correctly. You can also avoid the temptation of joining a review group, as many of them force authors to read a book which is not their usual genre of preference, which can result in a poor review. You want the correct reader to enjoy your book and to leave a review, this does not mean readers will never enjoy a book outside of their usual genre preference. There is a big debate that reviews are written for other readers, and not for the author to read. This is true but most authors will read reviews out of curiosity and excitement. Never respond to a bad review as it never ends well, I have witnessed other authors who have fallen into this trap. Potential customers are not stupid, they will be able to read between the lines. A great example is a bad review I once read for an adult book that once went viral across social media, a reader had given the book a 1 star review due to the heavy adult scenes. The book is an adult book, so the review was ridiculous. The front cover demonstrated that it was an adult book, the blurb pointed to a heavy adult content, yet the reader ignored all the signs. The obvious person in the wrong is the reader, and the author did not respond to some of the vile comments in the review. This is a great example for my earlier point, the reviews are for other readers and readers will read between the lines.

You will soon be bombarded with offers from readers with a large following on Instagram to review your book for a price, I have never done this before. I usually click on the persons profile and find a random popular post of theirs. On the surface the post may have thousands of likes, giving you the impression of a good way for you to reach new customers. I do a deep dive search and click on a few of the accounts that have liked the popular post, which usually reveals a fake or spam account. They are easy to spot as they usually only have a few followers or posts on their page. What is the point in paying a book reviewer to share a book review to their 100k followers if they have purchased the follows? Yes, you can buy followers but as I mentioned earlier, they are not real followers and are unlikely to ever buy your book. You could find a real account which a large following that is genuine, and if you want to use their services then the choice is yours.

Once you design and publish a website and your social media accounts, you will need to be vigilant of fake emails and offers. I receive offers for my books to be on sale at a festival in Germany at least once a month. The site is good, and convincing but they are indeed scammers. Be aware of this and research any offers or companies that approach you.

Social media accounts can help you build your following, spread your reputation and lead to book sales. Next, I will briefly explain if I achieved sales from the social medias I post on.

Facebook – I achieved sales, and this has increased since I opened an online shop for readers to buy directly from me.

Tik Tok – I have made sales.

Instagram – I have made sales.

Snapchat – I have made sales.

Bookroar – I have made sales.

X – I have made sales.

Goodreads & Bookbub – Unknown.

LinkedIn – I have made connections that have led to myself being published in an established author's book.

Website – Unknown.

YouTube – Unknown.

I have used the word unknown for sites that I cannot clearly pinpoint as the site of sale, this does not mean that it hasn't contributed to sales.

I post often across my social media sites, and this helps readers to find me, and for my books to reach a bigger audience.

The content I post varies between books I have read, my life, and author content. I use themes and post to coincide with world events, seasons, trending subjects and content. I use an app to make my videos, and I plan most of my picture content. I usually spend an hour making up ten or more videos for the month ahead. In-between my videos I share pictures and stories to keep followers engaged. Do keep in mind that social media platforms have a follow limit, currently I have reached my limit on Tik Tok, and I am close to the maximum on Instagram, so choose wisely when deciding which accounts to follow.

Chapter 7

Marketing is not a scary word, yet many authors fear it. I don't blame them; we all would rather use our energy being creative and passionate. I assume many authors fear the unknown, or the less desirable elements of the job. I previously mentioned that you could pay others to market your book but let's hope you have deep pockets for it is costly. No one will be more passionate or dedicated than you are, and no other person will understand your book and the characters better than you already do. My advice to any new author who is not confident with selling their book is for them to take a course on sales. The bottom line is your book is a product and you will need to sell it. You may try a soft approach or hard-hitting tactics, but the desired goal is always the same.

What is your fear when you think about marketing your book?

How can you improve the situation? Would you benefit from attending a sales class or author course?

Will reading a book on sales advice and marketing assist you?

Do you need to sign up for public speaking classes?

Is there a local writing group nearby that could help you with these fears?

Could you sign up for an author marketing course?

You are the first point of sale for most customers, whether that will be in person, at an event, or via social media.

Did I have experience in sales before I published my first book? Yes. I am an excellent salesperson.

Did I have enough knowledge for advertising books across social media, using Facebook and Amazon Adverts? No. I signed up to a course, and I read a few books for advice and help.

You may not be an expert in every section but there are plenty of authors who have trodden the path before you. The tools and knowledge you seek can be accessed, the decision you need to make is whether you will take advantage of the tools and resources available. A less desirable option which is selected by authors is for them to avoid developing their sales and marketing skills, leaving the success of their new book in fates hands.

I will break down various avenues for marketing your book and leave the big decision making up to you.

We discussed in a previous chapter that a cover artist can also make you promotional graphics, wonderful pictures for you to use to market your book.

Having pictures and ideas is a great starting point, but the best weapon you can have is a business plan. All successful businesses have one, and it is a great way for you to plan your marketing strategies.

Before you start composing your business plan you will need to know who your ideal reader is. If we know which type of customers will be interested in your book, you can pinpoint all avenues for finding them. For example, my second book is loved by spiritual people who are keen to read about paranormal experiences. My marketing plan involves me contacting Spiritual Churches, simply because my ideal readers hang out there. This is why it is vital to know the selling points and themes for your book so you can build a picture of your ideal reader.

Hang on. I don't really know what a business plan is!

A simple analogy is to imagine you are planning a wedding, you would write a list of all the tasks that you need to complete, with dates of when to complete each action by.

Your business plan will be a detailed plan of actions you will take to help the success of your book. The plan will include actions, dates, and marketing techniques. The plan can be for a short period of time or to cover the next five years. Making detailed notes of actions that you can make to help you achieve your goal. Your goal could be to sell books, but this goal is not specific. A more detailed goal could be for you to sell 1000 books within one year. The second goal is measurable, and therefore you will easily be able to know if you have achieved your target or not. You may wish to research the meaning of a business plan but to keep it simple it is a list of things to do. You can include goals, ideas, objectives, finances, marketing and strategies. A plan could also help you spot potential problems before they arise.

In my own business plan, I composed a list of all the different places I could sell my book or reach readers. My list varied from social media to local events, radio stations, newspapers, magazines, libraries, and churches. Each avenue was then assigned tasks for me to complete, some tasks required me to continually check up on actions. This will give you a plan to work from, and it will ensure that you do not miss any opportunities. In my plan I have set a task for me to contact local schools and offer my services to speak about my books, this is especially relevant on Love to Write Day, World Book

Day, and Mental Health Day. The opportunity of having access to hundreds of children could have been missed if I didn't already have the action in my plan.

You can design and make your own business plan by composing a list of all the places you could discuss or sell your book. Next, make a list of actions for you to do that will make sure you achieve these goals. Every goal should have an end date, this will give you time frames and measurable action dates. Follow your business plan and this will increase your chances of achieving more book sales. Another action in my business plan is for me to contact radio stations, I added a list of the most relevant stations nearby and then I sent them emails. I contact radio and newspaper stations every six months, and for me this has led to various live shows and articles being printed. All of this has given my books free advertisement and has surely added to book sales. I sign up to local events, selling my books and merchandise from a stall. This requires Public Liability Insurance and a Credit Card machine, all costs which are added to my accounts read for the end of tax year.

Once you have your detailed business plan, you won't need anything else! Instead of trolling posts on Facebook or Instagram looking for readers you can sit at your computer and action meaningful marketing tasks which are all aimed at the success of your book.

Let's do a recap, you have a book with promotional graphics, and a business plan. The plan will include marketing across social media and in person events with companies and readers. Next, we will break down some of the other segments of marketing.

Paid advertisement, via a media guru or paid adverts. Adverts are popular and they are an entity of their own, my advice is to attend a course or sign up for one online. I have used adverts across Facebook and Instagram, what I have discovered is that I usually earn back in royalties the amount of money I originally spent on the adverts. The sales help my books ranking and hopefully it earns me a few more reviews. I am yet to try Amazon adverts as I feel I need more knowledge, plus a change of lifestyle has decreased my finances making me unable to spare any cash for marketing adverts. You can ask for help and attend many courses but by simply experimenting you will find a winning formular for adverts on social media. I usually use a paid advert for my first book as this is the first in a series, which will hopefully lead onto further sales. Before Halloween I advertise my thriller book, which is usually successful in sales. You can use adverts to achieve page views, website visits, or new followers. I am a fan of new followers as I then have multiple opportunities to convince them to read my book. I fear that sharing any knowledge I have for the practical use of paid adverts could prove fruitless, because just like algorithms they change often. Many successful authors offer free courses online for using paid adverts, my advice is to take advantage of these opportunities before spending your hard-earned cash on paid advertising.

Radio and television stations could be a great way for you to advertise your book and reach thousands of readers. You may have a better outcome if you have a hook. I don't send emails begging them to let me appear on their show, I send them emails offering free books for them to giveaway. Local papers and tv shows are more likely to support you but think big and aim high. Buy newspapers or magazines and write down the contact details so you have a direct email list of potentially interested news outlets.

Shops and libraries are obvious places for readers to attend but do keep in mind that the big stores usually have shelves allocated and stocked for them. It is not always the manager who makes the decision for which books they stock and sell. You will have a higher chance of achieving a positive outcome if you target independent bookshops and smaller businesses.

Customers can request that libraries stock certain titles, fingers crossed that readers are asking for your book. You could donate a few copies of your book to the local library, a nice tactic and an easy way to make friends with the right contacts. A social media post about your donation gives your followers an idea of the kind of author you are. You could send marketing letters to shops, schools, and libraries, with the hope that they order and stock your book. If you have published with Ingram Spark then businesses can order directly from them, if not then you could try selling and stocking the books yourself.

In person events are a great way to speak with readers and spread the word about your new and exciting book. Join any groups that allows you to track local events, keeping you up to date with any community projects. Donating books as raffle prizes to local causes will increase your reputation, the choice is yours. Keep an eye out for community centre fayres, fetes, bookfairs, library events, school events, care home projects, and church events as all may offer the opportunity for you to have a stall.

Create your own event and invite customers to come and meet you! Find a shop or local business that will give you a space for free and set up a stall to sell your book. If you have access to money, then maybe book yourself as a stallholder and sign up to any event where you feel you might be successful. Personally, I seek Spiritual Fayres and Market Celebrations. I have held events in Wellbeing Shops, Schools, Churches and many other places. Many groups would love to meet an author, I often have success at WI groups or groups usually set up for retired people. There are hundreds of groups which meet up often, who would love the opportunity to have a guest speaker. A private event is my most profitable avenue, with the promise of a low payment for a few hours of my time but offering me the opportunity to sell my books afterwards to the group.

Another fabulous resource for you is to join a local writing group. I am fortunate enough to have found Portsmouth Author Collective, which was established by an author named Loree Westron. Loree is a traditionally published author who soon discovered that she would need to take the reins marketing her book, and the challenges us authors face. Portsmouth Author Collective was created for authors and writers to support each other, we do this via workshops, events, and marketing. It was via this supportive group that I have attended and delivered workshops, helping my knowledge and skills set grow alongside others. We share our skills and information to help each other sell and market our books.

I often sell my books via a stall at an event which we have paid for as a group, reducing our outgoings and increasing our opportunities for reaching new readers.

Do not lose faith if you attend an event and you do not make any money, at the beginning you will need to shout loud and make others aware of your book. I will share with you an interesting experience I had as a new author. I walked into Portsmouth library with a copy of my first book clasped tight in my hand. My partner had taken a photo of me stood outside the building ready to use for social media later that evening. As I approached the reception desk, I explained to the lady stationed there who I was, and that my book donation was expected from Mrs X who is the contact for the library. The receptionist pointed to an area at the back of the ground floor, a small wooden table with an allocation for books by local authors. I was excited and proud as I closed the gap between her and the table. My surroundings were in a blur as I gingerly placed my book onto the plastic shelfing. I soon was aware of a group of people behind me, curious of me as I snapped pictures of the book in its wonderful new home. A kind man asked me what I was doing, and I told him. I was placing my new book onto the shelf, and I needed photos for social media posts. The group were listening to our conversation while welcoming me with smiles. Unexpectedly one of them asked me to read them the blurb, and I froze with absolute excitement. After clearing my throat, I read to them loudly, and proudly the blurb of my book. As I looked around, I was greeted by at least twenty happy faces, who appeared impressed by my book's blurb. They asked me to read them some pages. My heart raced, and I couldn't believe it. I was a new author in my local library, reading my book to actual readers! I finished reading the page aloud and an applause erupted from my small gathering of listeners. The salesperson in me came to life and I started to reel off all the places they could buy my book. I was asked a final question of whether my book was available in audio, but I replied it wasn't yet an audio book. A silence fell over the group, until someone whispered, "We are a group of blind people." I stammered and stuttered, as there were no signs, canes or sunglasses dotted around. I left the library feeling like an idiot.

1 Year Later

I was at an event for local authors in a bookstore at Fratton, Portsmouth. An eager but shy young girl asked to speak with me as she wanted me to sign my second book, The Girl from Pompey: Conversations with the Dead! I asked her if she had read the first book, and she told me she had and she loved it. I am always asking readers how they heard about my books, so I popped the question to this young girl, who continued to tell me how she was recommended my book by her auntie that had heard me read when she was at a library group she attended for blind people! I love this story because it demonstrates that when you put positive energy out into the world it will always find its way back to you.

Another experience I would like to share with you is when I attended an event at a local college in Chichester. I paid £35 for my table, petrol money to drive there and I the obvious cost of my public liability insurance. It was a baking hot day, and I was seated under a glass roof. My table was positioned right next to the psychic readers stalls, making customers rush past me to give readers sat with customers some privacy. I sold two books and one bag the entire day. I was at a loss, not only did I not make any profit, but I had given up my one day off work that week to be there. However, I kept a smile on my face, and I interacted with others whenever I could. I decided to walk around the stall holders and give them all a business card, taking one of theirs in the process. I followed who I could on social media and tagged their businesses to help give them support, but I was a little disappointed. Twenty minutes before I was due to pack away my stall a gentleman approached me and asked me if I would like to be on his internet tv show. I was sceptical but we exchanged email addresses, and I left the event slightly disheartened but optimistic. A few weeks later I appeared live on his tv show discussing my books with his one million viewers. You will find reasons to feel like an event or an avenue didn't work out properly, but the truth is the only failure is for the ones we never truly explore. A failure is a lesson, and it might also be a fabulous opportunity. Do not be afraid to fail, you are just learning what not to do to succeed.

Book Launch Team verses a Book Launch Party!

A launch team are recruited as volunteers to share your posts across their social media, usually a few days before and on the day of a books release. The more people who share your posts the extra exposure your book will receive. I like to offer a free raffle for anyone who agrees to join my launch team, and I organise a video call for them to listen to a chapter ahead of the publication schedule.

A launch party is exactly what you would expect it to be. A party organised to celebrate your book release, you can make it a free event and sell copies of your book. You may choose to charge a ticket fee which includes access to a signed book and some freebies.

Both will help your book sales and reputation!

Lastly, I will mention your newsletter, building a newsletter list will give you access to warm leads for book promotion. You must give people the option to unsubscribe to your newsletter, and you can find new subscribers through your events, social media, and your website. I like to inform my subscribers of news before it is released to the public. I also like to offer them discounts and incentives, a nice reward for being a super fan. I send a newsletter every three or four months, I include new releases, projects, and a little about my life as an author.

Chapter 8

What is ALCS?

Authors Licensing and Collecting Society.

They are a fabulous company that collect royalty money owed to authors from secondary use. To simplify it, authors are paid primary royalties directly from publishing companies or from direct sale sites. ALCS was established by writers for writers, and they collect money from users who copy already distributed work. A great example is when libraries or schools may photocopy an article or book for use. Payments from ALCS are made in March and September, and they will deduct your one-off membership fee straight from your first payment.

Do you need to credit companies and professional people who have helped you to publish your book?

Yes, I always add the names of the cover designer, photographer, and editor. Most authors include this in the section of the book with your ISBN details.

When you upload a book to publish you can also add people who have professionally worked on your book, for example other authors, and artists. If you use a licensing free picture for your book, you do not have to credit them.

My biggest shock when I started publishing books is the friends and family who did not support me. It cost no money for others to support you on social media by engaging with your posts. Prepare yourself for this, as it may shock you. The positive side of this coin is the surprising friends or colleagues who will support you, when you never thought they would.

Use a diary to keep track of your events and special dates for marketing. When you walk into your local supermarket and you spot Christmas stock on the shelves in October, this is a clue for you to start your Christmas promotions. Businesses tend to work a few months ahead of time. In January I advertise books based on the new year and setting goals. I soon move onto Valentines Day gift posts, and then promotion for summer holiday reads. Towards the end of the summer, I concentrate on autumn or Halloween books, and then the Christmas posts start all over again. Throughout the year I have marked out dates for special occasions that may be useful for book promotions. The key takeaway from this is to plan and start promotions ahead of the specific date. If you are following a business plan, then this can be incorporated into it.

Take your time when it comes to the dreaded tasks of proof reading and try and leave a gap between writing a chapter and editing it. The human brain is a wonderful problem solver, which is why we can read words with missing letters and backward text. If you leave a gap between editing, then you are likely to spot mistakes more easily.

Be kind to yourself, all writers improve over time and evolve as will your books. With every book I write I learn and grow. Invest in a good computer and a comfy chair, you only have one back, so it is vital you take care of it.

Try to avoid comparing yourself to other authors, we are all different and travelling our own individual path. Success to one author may look very different to another. Readers can speed through several or more books a week, we are not in competition, there is enough space for us all. I teamed up with a local author who writes a similar genre to myself, and we take each other's books to events to sell. You may want to share posts to your followers for other authors books in a similar genre, in return for them sharing one of yours.

If readers do not know that your books are out there, they can't buy them. The first rule of marketing is to show up, be present and be available across different avenues. I share posts daily across social media and I still have friends asking me if I have published a book yet. Do not assume that your followers have seen that one post you shared, you will need to share frequently to ensure you have the highest exposure.

Readers are more likely to buy a book if they have an emotional response to a picture or post. Before you share a post or video with your followers ask yourself, how will this make others feel? Creating an urgency or call of action is a great way to self-promote books, make it clear what you would like them to do. Recently I posted a picture of my latest release, asking them to buy it now. My book was a few points away from hitting the bestseller list and I shared this news with them. In response they purchased my book. Followers, friends, and family will most likely have no idea how the publishing world works. Later, I posted a video thanking them for helping my book to hit the bestseller list. I also informed them specifically how they helped me, by sharing posts, engaging with posts, and by purchasing the book.

Imposter syndrome can come knocking at your door, which is common for most authors. There is an audience for your book, and lock away positive feedback to call upon when you need to.

Be patient, there is no timeline for success. A great way to understand this is to google top selling books of all time. Research the publication dates and then find the date when the book hit the bestseller list. It is interesting that some iconic books were released for many years before they were truly recognised. The Hobbit by J.R.R. Tolkien is still popular to this day and yet it was published in 1937. The Hobbit did not become a bestseller until the late 1960s.

Readers love a freebie and matching book merchandise, think about stocking bookmarks and keyrings, mugs, blankets, and any other bookish items you feel could be worth investing in.

Roller banners, business cards, and professional signage is always a great investment. I use table banners, and roller banners at events. It is not a coincidence that I stand in front of them when readers ask for a picture of me.

Business insurance is a must, especially if you are keen to attend events. My laptop recently died on me, and I had to find the money to replace it. I now have laptop cover, but I wish I had invested in it before my old one broke down.

Turn to others with experience and advice to share and utilise all avenues for support. You are not in this alone and the writing and author communities can be a great asset to you on your new journey.

When you publish a book, and you spot a mistake after it has been distributed DO NOT PANIC. It happens to us all, even the greatest books in the world are no stranger to typos and errors. You can easily rectify the manuscript and reupload it, in the meantime if customers order your book, they will receive the version with mistakes until your updated manuscript is approved.

Chapter 9

I am continuously asked what my secret to success is, and the truth is I appear more successful than what I truly am. I always aspire to be better and to do better. You will find many authors who are more established and successful than I am. I am not yet earning a six-figure salary from my author career. I do not have a budget for marketing, or an agent who has organised media coverage or book signings for me. Everything I have achieved is through my own creation, and for many self-published authors the journey to success is a slow one. For your average new author, they do not typically release a book and shoot to world success overnight. The path is different for us all, but most new authors struggle to build their brand, market their books, and keep motivated along the way. By having a true understanding of the industry, you can prepare yourself for the reality of the journey. You could be the minority, and after publishing a book you could become successful overnight. All authors hope for the best, but you must prepare for the other possibilities. When my first book was released, I thought I had achieved my goal. But instantly that goal was replaced with a new one for wanting to sell books. A short time after selling my book I then hoped it would hit the bestseller list. After my book hit the bestseller list, I then wanted to achieve more book reviews. As your book sales grow so will your aspirations and dreams.

On paper I sound fabulous, I have launched six books within a few years and three hit the bestseller list. I have my own book merchandise and clothing brand. I have appeared on television and radio often, with many articles being published about me and my books. When I walk down the street in my hometown people whisper to their friends, "That is Bryony Best, The Girl from Pompey." Established authors have included chapters about me in their books, tipping their hat to my success as a writer. I have been delivering workshops to help other authors and delivering mental-health sessions in schools to raise awareness. These achievements or facts do not accurately describe my journey. I will share the truth behind the scenes, firstly I achieved all the above while working five jobs. My workday started at 5am and I usually worked until 10pm in the evening. My life consisted of work and little to no social life. My few allocated sleeping hours consisted of me answering notifications on social media, and alarms set throughout the night for tasks that needed doing at a specific time. Majority of my following on Tik Tok is from the USA, making my optimized time for engagement to be silly o'clock in the morning. When I wasn't at my full-time employment, I was either marketing on social media, canvassing businesses for book sales, or attending an event. I used annual leave days from my main job to attend author events or radio interviews. Sometimes I would go months without a day off work. I am not sharing this with you to scare you, I am simply sharing my truthful experience of trying to build one career while still working in another. In the evenings I delivered workshops, and holistic therapy sessions to earn extra money. I needed extra finances to buy merchandise to sell at events, or books to sell in the select few local shops that I had chosen. My main job's salary paid my rent and bills, and the extra jobs helped to pay for the marketing signage, posters, cover designer, and ISBNs. I was fully aware that many new authors worked multiple jobs, and I am no stranger to running a business while also working full-time. I followed this regime for over three years, and where has it led me?

I am now working part-time for an employer and working part-time as an author. I have a better work-life balance, and my brand is growing stronger and stronger every day.

I am now in a position where I can prioritise my writing and put more effort into my author career. I chose to work hard, and I sacrificed my own social life to have the opportunity of a writing career. I am not suggesting that you copy my plan and give up your sleep, friends, and family in exchange for a writing career. I am sharing my experience to demonstrate the effort and lengths that it has taken me to achieve my goal. I could have put in less effort and time, and I would still have achieved my goal, it would have just taken a little longer. I have an A-type personality, and I run towards everything at 100 miles an hour. I do not know any other speed, and I am hypo-focused too.

When you are creating your goals in your business plan it is important to be realistic, consider which tasks and timeframes are achievable for you.

My secret to success was for me to enter my new career with a business plan, clear objectives, knowledge of the industry, and visualization. I made a vision board and hung it in clear view.

Be prepared, don't just write a book and hope for the best. Research the tasks and industry, learn new skills and take responsibility for your own success. Learn from others, make use of all free resources available. Your career as an author is a business, and readers are customers.

There are many authors who are not reaching the goals they set out to achieve, and many will confess that it is due to lack of effort and preparation.

Do you want to just be an author?

Or do you want to make a career out of writing books?

There is a big difference between the questions above and it is important you know the answer before you begin.

I wish you all the best in your writing career.

Bryony Best

Final Message to the Reader

I would like to thank you from the bottom of my heart for purchasing and reading this book. Please do consider reading my other publications.

I do ask, that you please take the time to leave a review on the site where you purchased this book and do also add your review to Goodreads - if you have an account with them.

Please upload a picture with your review to your social media platforms as this will help others to find my book.

Website   www.bryonybest.com

Sign up to my newsletter for rewards and exclusive discounts.

Twitter   @bryony_best

Instagram   @bestbryony

Facebook The Girl from Pompey

Tik Tok @bryonybest

Bryony Best

AUTHOR BIO

Bryony Best was born and raised in Portsmouth, United Kingdom. Currently residing in South Wales with her fiancé and her much loved Chihuahua dog named Luna. Bryony works as a Holistic Therapist, Author, and Life Coach. She lives a happy life of mindfulness and wellbeing. Bryony has previously published six books, and her aim is to become a full-time writer.

(The Girl from Pompey: Discovering the Key to Happiness and Fulfilment) Published - 2021

(The Girl from Pompey: Conversations with the Dead!) Published – 2022

(The Girl from Pompey: Bloodshed in the Hampshire Cabin) Published - 2023

(A Healing Journey: Healing the Body, Mind, and Spirit) Published – 2023

(The Girl from Pompey: Escaping the Rat Race) Published – 2024

(Poems and Nonsense: Creations from a Broken Mind) Published - 2024

Bryony's inspiration to share her stories with the world is to shine a light on mental health, and trauma healing. Since releasing her books, Bryony has become an advocate for mindfulness and wellbeing. Bryony delivers wellbeing workshops and courses for aspiring authors.

www.ingramcontent.com/pod-product-compliance
Lightning Source LLC
Chambersburg PA
CBHW052205070526
44585CB00017B/2071